Created and published by Knock Knock
Distributed by Who's There Inc.
Venice, CA 90291
knockknockstuff.com

© 2013 Who's There Inc.
All rights reserved
Knock Knock is a trademark of Who's There Inc.
Made in China

No part of this product may be used or reproduced in any manner
whatsoever without prior written permission from the publisher,
except in the case of brief quotations embodied in critical articles
and reviews. For information, address Knock Knock.

This book is a work of humor intended solely for entertainment purposes.
In no event will Knock Knock be liable to any reader for any damages,
including direct, indirect, incidental, special, consequential, or punitive
damages, arising out of or in connection with the use of the information
contained in this book. Harrumph.

Every reasonable attempt has been made to identify owners of copyright.
Errors or omissions will be corrected in subsequent editions.

Where specific company, product, and brand names are cited, copyright and
trademarks associated with these names are property of their respective owners.

ISBN: 978-160106452-3
UPC: 825703-50012-7

20 19 18 17 16 15 14 13 12 11 10 9 8 7 6

BATHROOM

Guest Book

Merry Christmas
to you & many
lovely visits
wished for your
guests!
♡ Rachel
Dec/2013

KNOCK
KNOCK®
VENICE, CALIFORNIA

Memorable Moments: _____

_____

_____

_____

_____

Additional Sentiments: _____

_____

_____

_____

_____

Welcome to My Bathroom

DATE OF VISIT: ....

TIME OF VISIT: .... AM / PM

SONG THAT BEST DESCRIBES THIS BATHROOM VISIT:

- ☐ "More Than a Feeling"
- ☐ "Push It"
- ☐ "The Sound of Silence"
- ☐ "Hurts So Good"
- ☐ "Blowin' in the Wind"
- ☐ "Good Vibrations"
- ☐ "Ring of Fire"
- ☐ ....

BATHROOM ACTIVITY BAR GRAPH

Shade in the amount of time spent on various activities.

A LONG TIME	
A LITTLE TIME	
NO TIME	
	SITTING ⋮ THINKING

SIGN IN, PLEASE

PURPOSE OF VISIT:

No. 1 .... No. 2 .... No. 3 ....

LOOKED IN MEDICINE CABINET?

☐ Yes, of course   ☐ No, of course not

BATHROOM DOODLE

☐ Crap   ☐ Not crap

LENGTH OF VISIT:

....

Hours   Minutes   Seconds

TIME SPENT GAZING IN MIRROR:

....

☐ Consciously   ☐ Unconsciously

THOUGHTS DURING THIS VISIT:

- ☐ The past   ☐ Business at hand
- ☐ The future   ☐ Other

REPORT CARD	A	B	C	D	F
Ambience					
Cleanliness					
Comfort					
Toilet Tissue					
Amenities					
Lighting					
Privacy					
OVERALL					

Memorable Moments: _____

_____

_____

_____

_____

_____

Additional Sentiments: _____

_____

_____

_____

_____

_____

Welcome to My Bathroom

DATE OF VISIT: ....

TIME OF VISIT: .... AM / PM

SONG THAT BEST DESCRIBES THIS BATHROOM VISIT:

☐ "More Than a Feeling"
☐ "Push It"
☐ "The Sound of Silence"
☐ "Hurts So Good"
☐ "Blowin' in the Wind"
☐ "Good Vibrations"
☐ "Ring of Fire"
☐ ....

BATHROOM ACTIVITY BAR GRAPH

Shade in the amount of time spent on various activities.

A LONG
TIME

A LITTLE
TIME

NO TIME

| SITTING | THINKING |

SIGN IN, PLEASE

PURPOSE OF VISIT:

No. 1 .... No. 2 .... No. 3 ....

LOOKED IN MEDICINE CABINET?

☐ Yes, of course   ☐ No, of course not

BATHROOM DOODLE

☐ Crap   ☐ Not crap

LENGTH OF VISIT:

....

Hours   Minutes   Seconds

TIME SPENT GAZING IN MIRROR:

....

☐ Consciously   ☐ Unconsciously

THOUGHTS DURING THIS VISIT:

☐ The past   ☐ Business at hand
☐ The future   ☐ Other

REPORT CARD	A	B	C	D	F
Ambience					
Cleanliness					
Comfort					
Toilet Tissue					
Amenities					
Lighting					
Privacy					
OVERALL					

Memorable Moments: _____

_____

_____

_____

_____

_____

Additional Sentiments: _____

_____

_____

_____

_____

_____

Welcome to My Bathroom

DATE OF VISIT: ....

TIME OF VISIT: .... AM / PM

SONG THAT BEST DESCRIBES THIS BATHROOM VISIT:

- ☐ "More Than a Feeling"
- ☐ "Push It"
- ☐ "The Sound of Silence"
- ☐ "Hurts So Good"
- ☐ "Blowin' in the Wind"
- ☐ "Good Vibrations"
- ☐ "Ring of Fire"
- ☐ ....

BATHROOM ACTIVITY BAR GRAPH

Shade in the amount of time spent on various activities.

A LONG TIME	
A LITTLE TIME	
NO TIME	
	SITTING : THINKING

SIGN IN, PLEASE

PURPOSE OF VISIT:

No. 1 .... No. 2 .... No. 3 ....

LOOKED IN MEDICINE CABINET?

☐ Yes, of course   ☐ No, of course not

BATHROOM DOODLE

☐ Crap   ☐ Not crap

LENGTH OF VISIT:

....

Hours   Minutes   Seconds

TIME SPENT GAZING IN MIRROR:

....

☐ Consciously   ☐ Unconsciously

THOUGHTS DURING THIS VISIT:

- ☐ The past
- ☐ The future
- ☐ Business at hand
- ☐ Other

REPORT CARD	A	B	C	D	F
Ambience					
Cleanliness					
Comfort					
Toilet Tissue					
Amenities					
Lighting					
Privacy					
OVERALL					

Memorable Moments: _____

_____

_____

_____

_____

Additional Sentiments: _____

_____

_____

_____

_____

Welcome to My Bathroom

DATE OF VISIT: ....

TIME OF VISIT: .... AM / PM

SONG THAT BEST DESCRIBES THIS BATHROOM VISIT:

- ☐ "More Than a Feeling"
- ☐ "Push It"
- ☐ "The Sound of Silence"
- ☐ "Hurts So Good"
- ☐ "Blowin' in the Wind"
- ☐ "Good Vibrations"
- ☐ "Ring of Fire"
- ☐ ....

BATHROOM ACTIVITY BAR GRAPH

Shade in the amount of time spent on various activities.

A LONG TIME	
A LITTLE TIME	
NO TIME	
	SITTING : THINKING

SIGN IN, PLEASE

PURPOSE OF VISIT:

No. 1 .... No. 2 .... No. 3 ....

LOOKED IN MEDICINE CABINET?

☐ Yes, of course   ☐ No, of course not

BATHROOM DOODLE

☐ Crap   ☐ Not crap

LENGTH OF VISIT:

....

Hours   Minutes   Seconds

TIME SPENT GAZING IN MIRROR:

....

☐ Consciously   ☐ Unconsciously

THOUGHTS DURING THIS VISIT:

- ☐ The past   ☐ Business at hand
- ☐ The future   ☐ Other

REPORT CARD	A	B	C	D	F
Ambience					
Cleanliness					
Comfort					
Toilet Tissue					
Amenities					
Lighting					
Privacy					
OVERALL					

Memorable Moments: _____

_____

_____

_____

_____

_____

Additional Sentiments: _____

_____

_____

_____

_____

_____

Welcome to My Bathroom

DATE OF VISIT: ....

TIME OF VISIT: .... AM / PM

SONG THAT BEST DESCRIBES THIS BATHROOM VISIT:

☐ "More Than a Feeling"
☐ "Push It"
☐ "The Sound of Silence"
☐ "Hurts So Good"
☐ "Blowin' in the Wind"
☐ "Good Vibrations"
☐ "Ring of Fire"
☐ ....

BATHROOM ACTIVITY BAR GRAPH

Shade in the amount of time spent on various activities.

A LONG TIME

A LITTLE TIME

NO TIME

SITTING   THINKING

SIGN IN, PLEASE

PURPOSE OF VISIT:

No. 1 ....   No. 2 ....   No. 3 ....

LOOKED IN MEDICINE CABINET?

☐ Yes, of course   ☐ No, of course not

BATHROOM DOODLE

☐ Crap   ☐ Not crap

LENGTH OF VISIT:

....

Hours   Minutes   Seconds

TIME SPENT GAZING IN MIRROR:

....

☐ Consciously   ☐ Unconsciously

THOUGHTS DURING THIS VISIT:

☐ The past   ☐ Business at hand
☐ The future   ☐ Other

REPORT CARD	A	B	C	D	F
Ambience					
Cleanliness					
Comfort					
Toilet Tissue					
Amenities					
Lighting					
Privacy					
OVERALL					

Memorable Moments: _____

_____

_____

_____

_____

_____

Additional Sentiments: _____

_____

_____

_____

_____

_____

Welcome to My Bathroom

DATE OF VISIT: ....

TIME OF VISIT: .... AM / PM

SONG THAT BEST DESCRIBES THIS BATHROOM VISIT:

- ☐ "More Than a Feeling"
- ☐ "Push It"
- ☐ "The Sound of Silence"
- ☐ "Hurts So Good"
- ☐ "Blowin' in the Wind"
- ☐ "Good Vibrations"
- ☐ "Ring of Fire"
- ☐ ....

BATHROOM ACTIVITY BAR GRAPH

Shade in the amount of time spent on various activities.

A LONG TIME	
A LITTLE TIME	
NO TIME	
	SITTING : THINKING

SIGN IN, PLEASE

PURPOSE OF VISIT:

No. 1 .... No. 2 .... No. 3 ....

LOOKED IN MEDICINE CABINET?

☐ Yes, of course   ☐ No, of course not

BATHROOM DOODLE

☐ Crap   ☐ Not crap

LENGTH OF VISIT:

....

Hours   Minutes   Seconds

TIME SPENT GAZING IN MIRROR:

....

☐ Consciously   ☐ Unconsciously

THOUGHTS DURING THIS VISIT:

- ☐ The past   ☐ Business at hand
- ☐ The future   ☐ Other

REPORT CARD	A	B	C	D	F
Ambience					
Cleanliness					
Comfort					
Toilet Tissue					
Amenities					
Lighting					
Privacy					
OVERALL					

Memorable Moments: _____

_____

_____

_____

_____

_____

Additional Sentiments: _____

_____

_____

_____

_____

_____

Welcome to My Bathroom

DATE OF VISIT: ....

TIME OF VISIT: .... AM / PM

SONG THAT BEST DESCRIBES THIS BATHROOM VISIT:

☐ "More Than a Feeling"
☐ "Push It"
☐ "The Sound of Silence"
☐ "Hurts So Good"
☐ "Blowin' in the Wind"
☐ "Good Vibrations"
☐ "Ring of Fire"
☐ ....

BATHROOM ACTIVITY BAR GRAPH
Shade in the amount of time spent on various activities.

A LONG TIME

A LITTLE TIME

NO TIME

| SITTING | THINKING |

SIGN IN, PLEASE

PURPOSE OF VISIT:

No. 1 ....   No. 2 ....   No. 3 ....

LOOKED IN MEDICINE CABINET?

☐ Yes, of course   ☐ No, of course not

BATHROOM DOODLE

☐ Crap   ☐ Not crap

LENGTH OF VISIT:

....

Hours   Minutes   Seconds

TIME SPENT GAZING IN MIRROR:

....

☐ Consciously   ☐ Unconsciously

THOUGHTS DURING THIS VISIT:

☐ The past   ☐ Business at hand
☐ The future   ☐ Other

REPORT CARD	A	B	C	D	F
Ambience					
Cleanliness					
Comfort					
Toilet Tissue					
Amenities					
Lighting					
Privacy					
OVERALL					

Memorable Moments: _____

_____

_____

_____

_____

_____

Additional Sentiments: _____

_____

_____

_____

_____

_____

Welcome to My Bathroom

DATE OF VISIT: ....

TIME OF VISIT: .... AM / PM

SONG THAT BEST DESCRIBES THIS BATHROOM VISIT:

- ☐ "More Than a Feeling"
- ☐ "Push It"
- ☐ "The Sound of Silence"
- ☐ "Hurts So Good"
- ☐ "Blowin' in the Wind"
- ☐ "Good Vibrations"
- ☐ "Ring of Fire"
- ☐ ....

BATHROOM ACTIVITY BAR GRAPH

Shade in the amount of time spent on various activities.

A LONG TIME

A LITTLE TIME

NO TIME

SITTING | THINKING

SIGN IN, PLEASE

PURPOSE OF VISIT:

No. 1 .... No. 2 .... No. 3 ....

LOOKED IN MEDICINE CABINET?

☐ Yes, of course ☐ No, of course not

BATHROOM DOODLE

☐ Crap ☐ Not crap

LENGTH OF VISIT:

....

Hours   Minutes   Seconds

TIME SPENT GAZING IN MIRROR:

....

☐ Consciously ☐ Unconsciously

THOUGHTS DURING THIS VISIT:

- ☐ The past   ☐ Business at hand
- ☐ The future   ☐ Other

REPORT CARD	A	B	C	D	F
Ambience					
Cleanliness					
Comfort					
Toilet Tissue					
Amenities					
Lighting					
Privacy					
OVERALL					

Memorable Moments: _____

_____

_____

_____

_____

_____

Additional Sentiments: _____

_____

_____

_____

_____

_____

Welcome to My Bathroom

DATE OF VISIT: ....

TIME OF VISIT: .... AM / PM

SONG THAT BEST DESCRIBES THIS BATHROOM VISIT:

- ☐ "More Than a Feeling"
- ☐ "Push It"
- ☐ "The Sound of Silence"
- ☐ "Hurts So Good"
- ☐ "Blowin' in the Wind"
- ☐ "Good Vibrations"
- ☐ "Ring of Fire"
- ☐ ....

BATHROOM ACTIVITY BAR GRAPH

Shade in the amount of time spent on various activities.

A LONG TIME	
A LITTLE TIME	
NO TIME	
	SITTING : THINKING

SIGN IN, PLEASE

PURPOSE OF VISIT:

No. 1 .... No. 2 .... No. 3 ....

LOOKED IN MEDICINE CABINET?

☐ Yes, of course   ☐ No, of course not

BATHROOM DOODLE

☐ Crap   ☐ Not crap

LENGTH OF VISIT:

....

Hours   Minutes   Seconds

TIME SPENT GAZING IN MIRROR:

....

☐ Consciously   ☐ Unconsciously

THOUGHTS DURING THIS VISIT:

- ☐ The past
- ☐ The future
- ☐ Business at hand
- ☐ Other

REPORT CARD	A	B	C	D	F
Ambience					
Cleanliness					
Comfort					
Toilet Tissue					
Amenities					
Lighting					
Privacy					
OVERALL					

Memorable Moments: _____

_____

_____

_____

_____

_____

Additional Sentiments: _____

_____

_____

_____

_____

_____

Welcome to My Bathroom

DATE OF VISIT: ....

TIME OF VISIT: .... AM / PM

SONG THAT BEST DESCRIBES THIS BATHROOM VISIT:

- ☐ "More Than a Feeling"
- ☐ "Push It"
- ☐ "The Sound of Silence"
- ☐ "Hurts So Good"
- ☐ "Blowin' in the Wind"
- ☐ "Good Vibrations"
- ☐ "Ring of Fire"
- ☐ ....

BATHROOM ACTIVITY BAR GRAPH

Shade in the amount of time spent on various activities.

	SITTING	THINKING
A LONG TIME		
A LITTLE TIME		
NO TIME		

SIGN IN, PLEASE

PURPOSE OF VISIT:

No. 1 .... No. 2 .... No. 3 ....

LOOKED IN MEDICINE CABINET?

☐ Yes, of course   ☐ No, of course not

BATHROOM DOODLE

☐ Crap   ☐ Not crap

LENGTH OF VISIT:

....

Hours   Minutes   Seconds

TIME SPENT GAZING IN MIRROR:

....

☐ Consciously   ☐ Unconsciously

THOUGHTS DURING THIS VISIT:

- ☐ The past   ☐ Business at hand
- ☐ The future   ☐ Other

REPORT CARD	A	B	C	D	F
Ambience					
Cleanliness					
Comfort					
Toilet Tissue					
Amenities					
Lighting					
Privacy					
OVERALL					

Memorable Moments: _____

_____

_____

_____

_____

_____

Additional Sentiments: _____

_____

_____

_____

_____

_____

Welcome to My Bathroom

DATE OF VISIT: ....

TIME OF VISIT: .... AM / PM

SONG THAT BEST DESCRIBES THIS BATHROOM VISIT:

☐ "More Than a Feeling"
☐ "Push It"
☐ "The Sound of Silence"
☐ "Hurts So Good"
☐ "Blowin' in the Wind"
☐ "Good Vibrations"
☐ "Ring of Fire"
☐ ....

BATHROOM ACTIVITY BAR GRAPH
Shade in the amount of time spent on various activities.

A LONG TIME	
A LITTLE TIME	
NO TIME	
	SITTING : THINKING

SIGN IN, PLEASE

PURPOSE OF VISIT:

No. 1 .... No. 2 .... No. 3 ....

LOOKED IN MEDICINE CABINET?

☐ Yes, of course   ☐ No, of course not

BATHROOM DOODLE

☐ Crap   ☐ Not crap

LENGTH OF VISIT:

....

Hours   Minutes   Seconds

TIME SPENT GAZING IN MIRROR:

....

☐ Consciously   ☐ Unconsciously

THOUGHTS DURING THIS VISIT:

☐ The past   ☐ Business at hand
☐ The future   ☐ Other

REPORT CARD	A	B	C	D	F
Ambience					
Cleanliness					
Comfort					
Toilet Tissue					
Amenities					
Lighting					
Privacy					
OVERALL					

Memorable Moments: _____

_____

_____

_____

_____

_____

Additional Sentiments: _____

_____

_____

_____

_____

_____

Welcome to My Bathroom

DATE OF VISIT: ....

TIME OF VISIT: .... AM / PM

SONG THAT BEST DESCRIBES THIS BATHROOM VISIT:

- ☐ "More Than a Feeling"
- ☐ "Push It"
- ☐ "The Sound of Silence"
- ☐ "Hurts So Good"
- ☐ "Blowin' in the Wind"
- ☐ "Good Vibrations"
- ☐ "Ring of Fire"
- ☐ ....

BATHROOM ACTIVITY BAR GRAPH

Shade in the amount of time spent on various activities.

A LONG TIME

A LITTLE TIME

NO TIME

| SITTING | THINKING |

SIGN IN, PLEASE

PURPOSE OF VISIT:

No. 1 .... No. 2 .... No. 3 ....

LOOKED IN MEDICINE CABINET?

☐ Yes, of course   ☐ No, of course not

BATHROOM DOODLE

☐ Crap   ☐ Not crap

LENGTH OF VISIT:

....

Hours   Minutes   Seconds

TIME SPENT GAZING IN MIRROR:

....

☐ Consciously   ☐ Unconsciously

THOUGHTS DURING THIS VISIT:

- ☐ The past
- ☐ The future
- ☐ Business at hand
- ☐ Other

REPORT CARD	A	B	C	D	F
Ambience					
Cleanliness					
Comfort					
Toilet Tissue					
Amenities					
Lighting					
Privacy					
OVERALL					

Memorable Moments: _____

_____

_____

_____

_____

_____

Additional Sentiments: _____

_____

_____

_____

_____

_____

Welcome to My Bathroom

DATE OF VISIT: ....

TIME OF VISIT: .... AM / PM

SIGN IN, PLEASE

LENGTH OF VISIT:

....

Hours   Minutes   Seconds

SONG THAT BEST DESCRIBES THIS BATHROOM VISIT:

- ☐ "More Than a Feeling"
- ☐ "Push It"
- ☐ "The Sound of Silence"
- ☐ "Hurts So Good"
- ☐ "Blowin' in the Wind"
- ☐ "Good Vibrations"
- ☐ "Ring of Fire"
- ☐ ....

PURPOSE OF VISIT:

No. 1 .... No. 2 .... No. 3 ....

LOOKED IN MEDICINE CABINET?

☐ Yes, of course   ☐ No, of course not

TIME SPENT GAZING IN MIRROR:

....

☐ Consciously   ☐ Unconsciously

THOUGHTS DURING THIS VISIT:

☐ The past   ☐ Business at hand
☐ The future   ☐ Other

BATHROOM DOODLE

BATHROOM ACTIVITY BAR GRAPH

Shade in the amount of time spent on various activities.

A LONG TIME

A LITTLE TIME

NO TIME

SITTING   THINKING

☐ Crap   ☐ Not crap

REPORT CARD	A	B	C	D	F
Ambience					
Cleanliness					
Comfort					
Toilet Tissue					
Amenities					
Lighting					
Privacy					
OVERALL					

Memorable Moments: _____
_____
_____
_____
_____

Additional Sentiments: _____
_____
_____
_____
_____

Welcome to My Bathroom

DATE OF VISIT: ....

TIME OF VISIT: .... AM / PM

SONG THAT BEST DESCRIBES THIS BATHROOM VISIT:

☐ "More Than a Feeling"
☐ "Push It"
☐ "The Sound of Silence"
☐ "Hurts So Good"
☐ "Blowin' in the Wind"
☐ "Good Vibrations"
☐ "Ring of Fire"
☐ ....

BATHROOM ACTIVITY BAR GRAPH

Shade in the amount of time spent on various activities.

A LONG TIME		
A LITTLE TIME		
NO TIME		
	SITTING	THINKING

SIGN IN, PLEASE

PURPOSE OF VISIT:

No. 1 .... No. 2 .... No. 3 ....

LOOKED IN MEDICINE CABINET?

☐ Yes, of course   ☐ No, of course not

BATHROOM DOODLE

☐ Crap   ☐ Not crap

LENGTH OF VISIT:

....
Hours   Minutes   Seconds

TIME SPENT GAZING IN MIRROR:

....

☐ Consciously   ☐ Unconsciously

THOUGHTS DURING THIS VISIT:

☐ The past   ☐ Business at hand
☐ The future   ☐ Other

REPORT CARD	A	B	C	D	F
Ambience					
Cleanliness					
Comfort					
Toilet Tissue					
Amenities					
Lighting					
Privacy					
OVERALL					

Memorable Moments: _____

_____

_____

_____

_____

_____

Additional Sentiments: _____

_____

_____

_____

_____

_____

Welcome to My Bathroom

DATE OF VISIT: ....

TIME OF VISIT: .... AM / PM

SONG THAT BEST DESCRIBES THIS BATHROOM VISIT:

- ☐ "More Than a Feeling"
- ☐ "Push It"
- ☐ "The Sound of Silence"
- ☐ "Hurts So Good"
- ☐ "Blowin' in the Wind"
- ☐ "Good Vibrations"
- ☐ "Ring of Fire"
- ☐ ....

BATHROOM ACTIVITY BAR GRAPH

Shade in the amount of time spent on various activities.

A LONG TIME

A LITTLE TIME

NO TIME

| SITTING | THINKING |

SIGN IN, PLEASE

PURPOSE OF VISIT:

No. 1 .... No. 2 .... No. 3 ....

LOOKED IN MEDICINE CABINET?

☐ Yes, of course ☐ No, of course not

BATHROOM DOODLE

☐ Crap ☐ Not crap

LENGTH OF VISIT:

....

Hours   Minutes   Seconds

TIME SPENT GAZING IN MIRROR:

....

☐ Consciously ☐ Unconsciously

THOUGHTS DURING THIS VISIT:

- ☐ The past   ☐ Business at hand
- ☐ The future   ☐ Other

REPORT CARD	A	B	C	D	F
Ambience					
Cleanliness					
Comfort					
Toilet Tissue					
Amenities					
Lighting					
Privacy					
OVERALL					

Memorable Moments: _____

_____

_____

_____

_____

Additional Sentiments: _____

_____

_____

_____

_____

Welcome to My Bathroom

DATE OF VISIT: ....

TIME OF VISIT: .... AM / PM

SONG THAT BEST DESCRIBES THIS BATHROOM VISIT:

- ☐ "More Than a Feeling"
- ☐ "Push It"
- ☐ "The Sound of Silence"
- ☐ "Hurts So Good"
- ☐ "Blowin' in the Wind"
- ☐ "Good Vibrations"
- ☐ "Ring of Fire"
- ☐ ....

BATHROOM ACTIVITY BAR GRAPH
Shade in the amount of time spent on various activities.

A LONG TIME		
A LITTLE TIME		
NO TIME		
	SITTING	THINKING

SIGN IN, PLEASE

PURPOSE OF VISIT:

No. 1 ....   No. 2 ....   No. 3 ....

LOOKED IN MEDICINE CABINET?

☐ Yes, of course   ☐ No, of course not

BATHROOM DOODLE

☐ Crap   ☐ Not crap

LENGTH OF VISIT:

....

Hours   Minutes   Seconds

TIME SPENT GAZING IN MIRROR:

....

☐ Consciously   ☐ Unconsciously

THOUGHTS DURING THIS VISIT:

- ☐ The past   ☐ Business at hand
- ☐ The future   ☐ Other

REPORT CARD	A	B	C	D	F
Ambience					
Cleanliness					
Comfort					
Toilet Tissue					
Amenities					
Lighting					
Privacy					
OVERALL					

Memorable Moments: _____

_____

_____

_____

_____

_____

Additional Sentiments: _____

_____

_____

_____

_____

_____

Welcome to My Bathroom

DATE OF VISIT: ....

TIME OF VISIT: .... AM / PM

SONG THAT BEST DESCRIBES THIS BATHROOM VISIT:

☐ "More Than a Feeling"
☐ "Push It"
☐ "The Sound of Silence"
☐ "Hurts So Good"
☐ "Blowin' in the Wind"
☐ "Good Vibrations"
☐ "Ring of Fire"
☐ ....

BATHROOM ACTIVITY BAR GRAPH
Shade in the amount of time spent on various activities.

A LONG TIME

A LITTLE TIME

NO TIME

| SITTING | THINKING |

SIGN IN, PLEASE

PURPOSE OF VISIT:

No. 1 .... No. 2 .... No. 3 ....

LOOKED IN MEDICINE CABINET?

☐ Yes, of course   ☐ No, of course not

BATHROOM DOODLE

☐ Crap   ☐ Not crap

LENGTH OF VISIT:

....

Hours   Minutes   Seconds

TIME SPENT GAZING IN MIRROR:

....

☐ Consciously   ☐ Unconsciously

THOUGHTS DURING THIS VISIT:

☐ The past   ☐ Business at hand
☐ The future   ☐ Other

REPORT CARD	A	B	C	D	F
Ambience					
Cleanliness					
Comfort					
Toilet Tissue					
Amenities					
Lighting					
Privacy					
OVERALL					

Memorable Moments: _____

_____

_____

_____

_____

Additional Sentiments: _____

_____

_____

_____

_____

Welcome to My Bathroom

DATE OF VISIT: ....

TIME OF VISIT: .... AM / PM

SONG THAT BEST DESCRIBES THIS BATHROOM VISIT:

☐ "More Than a Feeling"
☐ "Push It"
☐ "The Sound of Silence"
☐ "Hurts So Good"
☐ "Blowin' in the Wind"
☐ "Good Vibrations"
☐ "Ring of Fire"
☐ ....

BATHROOM ACTIVITY BAR GRAPH
Shade in the amount of time spent on various activities.

A LONG TIME

A LITTLE TIME

NO TIME

| SITTING | THINKING |

SIGN IN, PLEASE

PURPOSE OF VISIT:

No. 1 .... No. 2 .... No. 3 ....

LOOKED IN MEDICINE CABINET?

☐ Yes, of course ☐ No, of course not

BATHROOM DOODLE

☐ Crap ☐ Not crap

LENGTH OF VISIT:

....
Hours   Minutes   Seconds

TIME SPENT GAZING IN MIRROR:

....
☐ Consciously ☐ Unconsciously

THOUGHTS DURING THIS VISIT:
☐ The past   ☐ Business at hand
☐ The future   ☐ Other

REPORT CARD	A	B	C	D	F
Ambience					
Cleanliness					
Comfort					
Toilet Tissue					
Amenities					
Lighting					
Privacy					
OVERALL					

Memorable Moments: _____

_____

_____

_____

_____

Additional Sentiments: _____

_____

_____

_____

_____

Welcome to My Bathroom

DATE OF VISIT: ....

TIME OF VISIT: .... AM / PM

SONG THAT BEST DESCRIBES THIS BATHROOM VISIT:

☐ "More Than a Feeling"
☐ "Push It"
☐ "The Sound of Silence"
☐ "Hurts So Good"
☐ "Blowin' in the Wind"
☐ "Good Vibrations"
☐ "Ring of Fire"
☐ ....

BATHROOM ACTIVITY BAR GRAPH
Shade in the amount of time spent on various activities.

A LONG TIME

A LITTLE TIME

NO TIME

| SITTING | THINKING |

SIGN IN, PLEASE

PURPOSE OF VISIT:

No. 1 .... No. 2 .... No. 3 ....

LOOKED IN MEDICINE CABINET?

☐ Yes, of course   ☐ No, of course not

BATHROOM DOODLE

☐ Crap   ☐ Not crap

LENGTH OF VISIT:

....

Hours   Minutes   Seconds

TIME SPENT GAZING IN MIRROR:

....

☐ Consciously   ☐ Unconsciously

THOUGHTS DURING THIS VISIT:

☐ The past   ☐ Business at hand
☐ The future   ☐ Other

REPORT CARD	A	B	C	D	F
Ambience					
Cleanliness					
Comfort					
Toilet Tissue					
Amenities					
Lighting					
Privacy					
OVERALL					

Memorable Moments: _____

_____

_____

_____

_____

_____

Additional Sentiments: _____

_____

_____

_____

_____

_____

Welcome to My Bathroom

DATE OF VISIT: ....

TIME OF VISIT: .... AM / PM

SONG THAT BEST DESCRIBES THIS BATHROOM VISIT:

☐ "More Than a Feeling"
☐ "Push It"
☐ "The Sound of Silence"
☐ "Hurts So Good"
☐ "Blowin' in the Wind"
☐ "Good Vibrations"
☐ "Ring of Fire"
☐ ....

BATHROOM ACTIVITY BAR GRAPH

Shade in the amount of time spent on various activities.

A LONG TIME

A LITTLE TIME

NO TIME

SITTING | THINKING

SIGN IN, PLEASE

PURPOSE OF VISIT:

No. 1 .... No. 2 .... No. 3 ....

LOOKED IN MEDICINE CABINET?

☐ Yes, of course   ☐ No, of course not

BATHROOM DOODLE

☐ Crap   ☐ Not crap

LENGTH OF VISIT:

....

Hours   Minutes   Seconds

TIME SPENT GAZING IN MIRROR:

....

☐ Consciously   ☐ Unconsciously

THOUGHTS DURING THIS VISIT:

☐ The past   ☐ Business at hand
☐ The future   ☐ Other

REPORT CARD	A	B	C	D	F
Ambience					
Cleanliness					
Comfort					
Toilet Tissue					
Amenities					
Lighting					
Privacy					
OVERALL					

Memorable Moments: _____

_____

_____

_____

_____

_____

Additional Sentiments: _____

_____

_____

_____

_____

Welcome to My Bathroom

DATE OF VISIT: ....

TIME OF VISIT: .... AM / PM

SIGN IN, PLEASE

LENGTH OF VISIT:

....

Hours   Minutes   Seconds

SONG THAT BEST DESCRIBES THIS BATHROOM VISIT:

☐ "More Than a Feeling"
☐ "Push It"
☐ "The Sound of Silence"
☐ "Hurts So Good"
☐ "Blowin' in the Wind"
☐ "Good Vibrations"
☐ "Ring of Fire"
☐ ....

PURPOSE OF VISIT:

No. 1 .... No. 2 .... No. 3 ....

LOOKED IN MEDICINE CABINET?

☐ Yes, of course   ☐ No, of course not

BATHROOM DOODLE

TIME SPENT GAZING IN MIRROR:

....

☐ Consciously   ☐ Unconsciously

THOUGHTS DURING THIS VISIT:

☐ The past   ☐ Business at hand
☐ The future   ☐ Other

BATHROOM ACTIVITY BAR GRAPH
Shade in the amount of time spent on various activities.

A LONG TIME

A LITTLE TIME

NO TIME

SITTING | THINKING

☐ Crap   ☐ Not crap

REPORT CARD	A	B	C	D	F
Ambience					
Cleanliness					
Comfort					
Toilet Tissue					
Amenities					
Lighting					
Privacy					
OVERALL					

Memorable Moments: _____

_____

_____

_____

_____

_____

Additional Sentiments: _____

_____

_____

_____

_____

_____

Welcome to My Bathroom

DATE OF VISIT: ....

TIME OF VISIT: .... AM / PM

SONG THAT BEST DESCRIBES THIS BATHROOM VISIT:

- ☐ "More Than a Feeling"
- ☐ "Push It"
- ☐ "The Sound of Silence"
- ☐ "Hurts So Good"
- ☐ "Blowin' in the Wind"
- ☐ "Good Vibrations"
- ☐ "Ring of Fire"
- ☐ ....

BATHROOM ACTIVITY BAR GRAPH

Shade in the amount of time spent on various activities.

A LONG TIME

A LITTLE TIME

NO TIME

SITTING | THINKING

SIGN IN, PLEASE

PURPOSE OF VISIT:

No. 1 .... No. 2 .... No. 3 ....

LOOKED IN MEDICINE CABINET?

☐ Yes, of course ☐ No, of course not

BATHROOM DOODLE

☐ Crap   ☐ Not crap

LENGTH OF VISIT:

....

Hours   Minutes   Seconds

TIME SPENT GAZING IN MIRROR:

....

☐ Consciously   ☐ Unconsciously

THOUGHTS DURING THIS VISIT:

- ☐ The past
- ☐ The future
- ☐ Business at hand
- ☐ Other

REPORT CARD	A	B	C	D	F
Ambience					
Cleanliness					
Comfort					
Toilet Tissue					
Amenities					
Lighting					
Privacy					
OVERALL					

Memorable Moments: _____

_____

_____

_____

_____

_____

Additional Sentiments: _____

_____

_____

_____

_____

_____

Welcome to My Bathroom

DATE OF VISIT: ....

TIME OF VISIT: .... AM / PM

SONG THAT BEST DESCRIBES THIS BATHROOM VISIT:

- ☐ "More Than a Feeling"
- ☐ "Push It"
- ☐ "The Sound of Silence"
- ☐ "Hurts So Good"
- ☐ "Blowin' in the Wind"
- ☐ "Good Vibrations"
- ☐ "Ring of Fire"
- ☐ ....

BATHROOM ACTIVITY BAR GRAPH

Shade in the amount of time spent on various activities.

A LONG TIME	
A LITTLE TIME	
NO TIME	
	SITTING : THINKING

SIGN IN, PLEASE

PURPOSE OF VISIT:

No. 1 ....   No. 2 ....   No. 3 ....

LOOKED IN MEDICINE CABINET?

☐ Yes, of course   ☐ No, of course not

BATHROOM DOODLE

☐ Crap   ☐ Not crap

LENGTH OF VISIT:

....

Hours   Minutes   Seconds

TIME SPENT GAZING IN MIRROR:

....

☐ Consciously   ☐ Unconsciously

THOUGHTS DURING THIS VISIT:

- ☐ The past   ☐ Business at hand
- ☐ The future   ☐ Other

REPORT CARD	A	B	C	D	F
Ambience					
Cleanliness					
Comfort					
Toilet Tissue					
Amenities					
Lighting					
Privacy					
OVERALL					

Memorable Moments: _____

_____

_____

_____

_____

_____

Additional Sentiments: _____

_____

_____

_____

_____

_____

Welcome to My Bathroom

DATE OF VISIT: ....

TIME OF VISIT: .... AM / PM

SONG THAT BEST DESCRIBES THIS BATHROOM VISIT:

☐ "More Than a Feeling"
☐ "Push It"
☐ "The Sound of Silence"
☐ "Hurts So Good"
☐ "Blowin' in the Wind"
☐ "Good Vibrations"
☐ "Ring of Fire"
☐ ....

BATHROOM ACTIVITY BAR GRAPH
Shade in the amount of time spent on various activities.

A LONG TIME

A LITTLE TIME

NO TIME

| SITTING | THINKING |

SIGN IN, PLEASE

PURPOSE OF VISIT:

No. 1 .... No. 2 .... No. 3 ....

LOOKED IN MEDICINE CABINET?

☐ Yes, of course   ☐ No, of course not

BATHROOM DOODLE

☐ Crap   ☐ Not crap

LENGTH OF VISIT:

....

Hours   Minutes   Seconds

TIME SPENT GAZING IN MIRROR:

....

☐ Consciously   ☐ Unconsciously

THOUGHTS DURING THIS VISIT:

☐ The past   ☐ Business at hand
☐ The future   ☐ Other

REPORT CARD	A	B	C	D	F
Ambience					
Cleanliness					
Comfort					
Toilet Tissue					
Amenities					
Lighting					
Privacy					
OVERALL					

Memorable Moments: _____

_____

_____

_____

_____

_____

Additional Sentiments: _____

_____

_____

_____

_____

_____

Welcome to My Bathroom

DATE OF VISIT: ....

TIME OF VISIT: .... AM / PM

SONG THAT BEST DESCRIBES THIS BATHROOM VISIT:

- ☐ "More Than a Feeling"
- ☐ "Push It"
- ☐ "The Sound of Silence"
- ☐ "Hurts So Good"
- ☐ "Blowin' in the Wind"
- ☐ "Good Vibrations"
- ☐ "Ring of Fire"
- ☐ ....

BATHROOM ACTIVITY BAR GRAPH

Shade in the amount of time spent on various activities.

A LONG TIME	
A LITTLE TIME	
NO TIME	
	SITTING : THINKING

SIGN IN, PLEASE

PURPOSE OF VISIT:

No. 1 .... No. 2 .... No. 3 ....

LOOKED IN MEDICINE CABINET?

☐ Yes, of course   ☐ No, of course not

BATHROOM DOODLE

☐ Crap   ☐ Not crap

LENGTH OF VISIT:

....

Hours   Minutes   Seconds

TIME SPENT GAZING IN MIRROR:

....

☐ Consciously   ☐ Unconsciously

THOUGHTS DURING THIS VISIT:

- ☐ The past   ☐ Business at hand
- ☐ The future   ☐ Other

REPORT CARD	A	B	C	D	F
Ambience					
Cleanliness					
Comfort					
Toilet Tissue					
Amenities					
Lighting					
Privacy					
OVERALL					

Memorable Moments: _____

_____

_____

_____

_____

_____

Additional Sentiments: _____

_____

_____

_____

_____

_____

Welcome to My Bathroom

DATE OF VISIT: ....

TIME OF VISIT: .... AM / PM

SONG THAT BEST DESCRIBES THIS BATHROOM VISIT:

☐ "More Than a Feeling"
☐ "Push It"
☐ "The Sound of Silence"
☐ "Hurts So Good"
☐ "Blowin' in the Wind"
☐ "Good Vibrations"
☐ "Ring of Fire"
☐ ....

BATHROOM ACTIVITY BAR GRAPH
Shade in the amount of time spent on various activities.

A LONG TIME

A LITTLE TIME

NO TIME

| SITTING | THINKING |

SIGN IN, PLEASE

PURPOSE OF VISIT:

No. 1 .... No. 2 .... No. 3 ....

LOOKED IN MEDICINE CABINET?

☐ Yes, of course   ☐ No, of course not

BATHROOM DOODLE

☐ Crap   ☐ Not crap

LENGTH OF VISIT:

....

Hours   Minutes   Seconds

TIME SPENT GAZING IN MIRROR:

....

☐ Consciously   ☐ Unconsciously

THOUGHTS DURING THIS VISIT:

☐ The past   ☐ Business at hand
☐ The future   ☐ Other

REPORT CARD	A	B	C	D	F
Ambience					
Cleanliness					
Comfort					
Toilet Tissue					
Amenities					
Lighting					
Privacy					
OVERALL					

Memorable Moments: _____

_____

_____

_____

_____

_____

Additional Sentiments: _____

_____

_____

_____

_____

_____

Welcome to My Bathroom

DATE OF VISIT: ....

TIME OF VISIT: .... AM / PM

SONG THAT BEST DESCRIBES THIS BATHROOM VISIT:

- ☐ "More Than a Feeling"
- ☐ "Push It"
- ☐ "The Sound of Silence"
- ☐ "Hurts So Good"
- ☐ "Blowin' in the Wind"
- ☐ "Good Vibrations"
- ☐ "Ring of Fire"
- ☐ ....

BATHROOM ACTIVITY BAR GRAPH

Shade in the amount of time spent on various activities.

A LONG TIME

A LITTLE TIME

NO TIME

| SITTING | THINKING |

SIGN IN, PLEASE

PURPOSE OF VISIT:

No. 1 ....   No. 2 ....   No. 3 ....

LOOKED IN MEDICINE CABINET?

☐ Yes, of course   ☐ No, of course not

BATHROOM DOODLE

☐ Crap   ☐ Not crap

LENGTH OF VISIT:

....

Hours   Minutes   Seconds

TIME SPENT GAZING IN MIRROR:

....

☐ Consciously   ☐ Unconsciously

THOUGHTS DURING THIS VISIT:

☐ The past   ☐ Business at hand
☐ The future   ☐ Other

REPORT CARD	A	B	C	D	F
Ambience					
Cleanliness					
Comfort					
Toilet Tissue					
Amenities					
Lighting					
Privacy					
OVERALL					

Memorable Moments: _____

_____

_____

_____

_____

_____

Additional Sentiments: _____

_____

_____

_____

_____

_____

Welcome to My Bathroom

DATE OF VISIT: ....

TIME OF VISIT: .... AM / PM

SONG THAT BEST DESCRIBES THIS BATHROOM VISIT:

- ☐ "More Than a Feeling"
- ☐ "Push It"
- ☐ "The Sound of Silence"
- ☐ "Hurts So Good"
- ☐ "Blowin' in the Wind"
- ☐ "Good Vibrations"
- ☐ "Ring of Fire"
- ☐ ....

BATHROOM ACTIVITY BAR GRAPH

Shade in the amount of time spent on various activities.

A LONG TIME

A LITTLE TIME

NO TIME

| SITTING | THINKING |

SIGN IN, PLEASE

PURPOSE OF VISIT:

No. 1 .... No. 2 .... No. 3 ....

LOOKED IN MEDICINE CABINET?

☐ Yes, of course   ☐ No, of course not

BATHROOM DOODLE

☐ Crap   ☐ Not crap

LENGTH OF VISIT:

....

Hours   Minutes   Seconds

TIME SPENT GAZING IN MIRROR:

....

☐ Consciously   ☐ Unconsciously

THOUGHTS DURING THIS VISIT:

- ☐ The past   ☐ Business at hand
- ☐ The future   ☐ Other

REPORT CARD	A	B	C	D	F
Ambience					
Cleanliness					
Comfort					
Toilet Tissue					
Amenities					
Lighting					
Privacy					
OVERALL					

Memorable Moments: _____

_____

_____

_____

_____

_____

Additional Sentiments: _____

_____

_____

_____

_____

_____

Welcome to My Bathroom

DATE OF VISIT: ....

TIME OF VISIT: .... AM / PM

SONG THAT BEST DESCRIBES THIS BATHROOM VISIT:

- ☐ "More Than a Feeling"
- ☐ "Push It"
- ☐ "The Sound of Silence"
- ☐ "Hurts So Good"
- ☐ "Blowin' in the Wind"
- ☐ "Good Vibrations"
- ☐ "Ring of Fire"
- ☐ ....

BATHROOM ACTIVITY BAR GRAPH

Shade in the amount of time spent on various activities.

A LONG TIME	
A LITTLE TIME	
NO TIME	
	SITTING : THINKING

SIGN IN, PLEASE

PURPOSE OF VISIT:

No. 1 .... No. 2 .... No. 3 ....

LOOKED IN MEDICINE CABINET?

☐ Yes, of course   ☐ No, of course not

BATHROOM DOODLE

☐ Crap   ☐ Not crap

LENGTH OF VISIT:

....

Hours   Minutes   Seconds

TIME SPENT GAZING IN MIRROR:

....

☐ Consciously   ☐ Unconsciously

THOUGHTS DURING THIS VISIT:

- ☐ The past   ☐ Business at hand
- ☐ The future   ☐ Other

REPORT CARD	A	B	C	D	F
Ambience					
Cleanliness					
Comfort					
Toilet Tissue					
Amenities					
Lighting					
Privacy					
OVERALL					

Memorable Moments: _____

_____

_____

_____

_____

Additional Sentiments: _____

_____

_____

_____

_____

_____

Welcome to My Bathroom

DATE OF VISIT: ....

TIME OF VISIT: .... AM / PM

SONG THAT BEST DESCRIBES THIS BATHROOM VISIT:

- ☐ "More Than a Feeling"
- ☐ "Push It"
- ☐ "The Sound of Silence"
- ☐ "Hurts So Good"
- ☐ "Blowin' in the Wind"
- ☐ "Good Vibrations"
- ☐ "Ring of Fire"
- ☐ ....

BATHROOM ACTIVITY BAR GRAPH
Shade in the amount of time spent on various activities.

A LONG TIME

A LITTLE TIME

NO TIME

| SITTING | THINKING |

SIGN IN, PLEASE

PURPOSE OF VISIT:

No. 1 .... No. 2 .... No. 3 ....

LOOKED IN MEDICINE CABINET?

☐ Yes, of course   ☐ No, of course not

BATHROOM DOODLE

☐ Crap   ☐ Not crap

LENGTH OF VISIT:

....

Hours   Minutes   Seconds

TIME SPENT GAZING IN MIRROR:

....

☐ Consciously   ☐ Unconsciously

THOUGHTS DURING THIS VISIT:

- ☐ The past   ☐ Business at hand
- ☐ The future   ☐ Other

REPORT CARD	A	B	C	D	F
Ambience					
Cleanliness					
Comfort					
Toilet Tissue					
Amenities					
Lighting					
Privacy					
OVERALL					

Memorable Moments: _____

_____

_____

_____

_____

_____

Additional Sentiments: _____

_____

_____

_____

_____

_____

Welcome to My Bathroom

DATE OF VISIT: ....

TIME OF VISIT: .... AM / PM

SONG THAT BEST DESCRIBES THIS BATHROOM VISIT:
- ☐ "More Than a Feeling"
- ☐ "Push It"
- ☐ "The Sound of Silence"
- ☐ "Hurts So Good"
- ☐ "Blowin' in the Wind"
- ☐ "Good Vibrations"
- ☐ "Ring of Fire"
- ☐ ....

BATHROOM ACTIVITY BAR GRAPH
Shade in the amount of time spent on various activities.

A LONG TIME

A LITTLE TIME

NO TIME

SITTING | THINKING

SIGN IN, PLEASE

PURPOSE OF VISIT:

No. 1 .... No. 2 .... No. 3 ....

LOOKED IN MEDICINE CABINET?
☐ Yes, of course ☐ No, of course not

BATHROOM DOODLE

☐ Crap   ☐ Not crap

LENGTH OF VISIT:

....

Hours   Minutes   Seconds

TIME SPENT GAZING IN MIRROR:

....

☐ Consciously   ☐ Unconsciously

THOUGHTS DURING THIS VISIT:
- ☐ The past   ☐ Business at hand
- ☐ The future   ☐ Other

REPORT CARD	A	B	C	D	F
Ambience					
Cleanliness					
Comfort					
Toilet Tissue					
Amenities					
Lighting					
Privacy					
OVERALL					

Memorable Moments: _____

_____

_____

_____

_____

_____

Additional Sentiments: _____

_____

_____

_____

_____

_____

Welcome to My Bathroom

DATE OF VISIT: ....

TIME OF VISIT: .... AM / PM

SONG THAT BEST DESCRIBES THIS BATHROOM VISIT:

- ☐ "More Than a Feeling"
- ☐ "Push It"
- ☐ "The Sound of Silence"
- ☐ "Hurts So Good"
- ☐ "Blowin' in the Wind"
- ☐ "Good Vibrations"
- ☐ "Ring of Fire"
- ☐ ....

BATHROOM ACTIVITY BAR GRAPH

Shade in the amount of time spent on various activities.

A LONG TIME		
A LITTLE TIME		
NO TIME		
	SITTING	THINKING

SIGN IN, PLEASE

PURPOSE OF VISIT:

No. 1 .... No. 2 .... No. 3 ....

LOOKED IN MEDICINE CABINET?

☐ Yes, of course   ☐ No, of course not

BATHROOM DOODLE

☐ Crap   ☐ Not crap

LENGTH OF VISIT:

....

Hours   Minutes   Seconds

TIME SPENT GAZING IN MIRROR:

....

☐ Consciously   ☐ Unconsciously

THOUGHTS DURING THIS VISIT:

- ☐ The past
- ☐ The future
- ☐ Business at hand
- ☐ Other

REPORT CARD	A	B	C	D	F
Ambience					
Cleanliness					
Comfort					
Toilet Tissue					
Amenities					
Lighting					
Privacy					
OVERALL					

Memorable Moments: _____

_____

_____

_____

_____

Additional Sentiments: _____

_____

_____

_____

_____

Welcome to My Bathroom

DATE OF VISIT: ....

TIME OF VISIT: .... AM / PM

SONG THAT BEST DESCRIBES THIS BATHROOM VISIT:

☐ "More Than a Feeling"
☐ "Push It"
☐ "The Sound of Silence"
☐ "Hurts So Good"
☐ "Blowin' in the Wind"
☐ "Good Vibrations"
☐ "Ring of Fire"
☐ ....

BATHROOM ACTIVITY BAR GRAPH
Shade in the amount of time spent on various activities.

A LONG TIME	
A LITTLE TIME	
NO TIME	
	SITTING THINKING

SIGN IN, PLEASE

PURPOSE OF VISIT:

No. 1 .... No. 2 .... No. 3 ....

LOOKED IN MEDICINE CABINET?

☐ Yes, of course   ☐ No, of course not

BATHROOM DOODLE

☐ Crap   ☐ Not crap

LENGTH OF VISIT:

....
Hours   Minutes   Seconds

TIME SPENT GAZING IN MIRROR:

....

☐ Consciously   ☐ Unconsciously

THOUGHTS DURING THIS VISIT:

☐ The past   ☐ Business at hand
☐ The future   ☐ Other

REPORT CARD	A	B	C	D	F
Ambience					
Cleanliness					
Comfort					
Toilet Tissue					
Amenities					
Lighting					
Privacy					
OVERALL					

Memorable Moments: _____

_____

_____

_____

_____

Additional Sentiments: _____

_____

_____

_____

_____

Welcome to My Bathroom

DATE OF VISIT: ....

TIME OF VISIT: .... AM / PM

SONG THAT BEST DESCRIBES THIS BATHROOM VISIT:

- ☐ "More Than a Feeling"
- ☐ "Push It"
- ☐ "The Sound of Silence"
- ☐ "Hurts So Good"
- ☐ "Blowin' in the Wind"
- ☐ "Good Vibrations"
- ☐ "Ring of Fire"
- ☐ ....

BATHROOM ACTIVITY BAR GRAPH

Shade in the amount of time spent on various activities.

A LONG TIME		
A LITTLE TIME		
NO TIME		
	SITTING	THINKING

SIGN IN, PLEASE

PURPOSE OF VISIT:

No. 1 .... No. 2 .... No. 3 ....

LOOKED IN MEDICINE CABINET?

☐ Yes, of course ☐ No, of course not

BATHROOM DOODLE

☐ Crap ☐ Not crap

LENGTH OF VISIT:

....

Hours   Minutes   Seconds

TIME SPENT GAZING IN MIRROR:

....

☐ Consciously ☐ Unconsciously

THOUGHTS DURING THIS VISIT:

- ☐ The past ☐ Business at hand
- ☐ The future ☐ Other

REPORT CARD	A	B	C	D	F
Ambience					
Cleanliness					
Comfort					
Toilet Tissue					
Amenities					
Lighting					
Privacy					
OVERALL					

Memorable Moments: _____

_____

_____

_____

_____

_____

Additional Sentiments: _____

_____

_____

_____

_____

_____

Welcome to My Bathroom

DATE OF VISIT: ....

TIME OF VISIT: .... AM / PM

SONG THAT BEST DESCRIBES THIS BATHROOM VISIT:

- ☐ "More Than a Feeling"
- ☐ "Push It"
- ☐ "The Sound of Silence"
- ☐ "Hurts So Good"
- ☐ "Blowin' in the Wind"
- ☐ "Good Vibrations"
- ☐ "Ring of Fire"
- ☐ ....

BATHROOM ACTIVITY BAR GRAPH

Shade in the amount of time spent on various activities.

A LONG TIME

A LITTLE TIME

NO TIME

SITTING : THINKING

SIGN IN, PLEASE

PURPOSE OF VISIT:

No. 1 .... No. 2 .... No. 3 ....

LOOKED IN MEDICINE CABINET?

☐ Yes, of course   ☐ No, of course not

BATHROOM DOODLE

☐ Crap   ☐ Not crap

LENGTH OF VISIT:

....

Hours   Minutes   Seconds

TIME SPENT GAZING IN MIRROR:

....

☐ Consciously   ☐ Unconsciously

THOUGHTS DURING THIS VISIT:

- ☐ The past   ☐ Business at hand
- ☐ The future   ☐ Other

REPORT CARD	A	B	C	D	F
Ambience					
Cleanliness					
Comfort					
Toilet Tissue					
Amenities					
Lighting					
Privacy					
OVERALL					

Memorable Moments: _____

_____

_____

_____

_____

_____

Additional Sentiments: _____

_____

_____

_____

_____

Welcome to My Bathroom

DATE OF VISIT: ....

TIME OF VISIT: .... AM / PM

SONG THAT BEST DESCRIBES THIS BATHROOM VISIT:

- ☐ "More Than a Feeling"
- ☐ "Push It"
- ☐ "The Sound of Silence"
- ☐ "Hurts So Good"
- ☐ "Blowin' in the Wind"
- ☐ "Good Vibrations"
- ☐ "Ring of Fire"
- ☐ ....

BATHROOM ACTIVITY BAR GRAPH

Shade in the amount of time spent on various activities.

A LONG TIME

A LITTLE TIME

NO TIME

| SITTING | THINKING |

SIGN IN, PLEASE

PURPOSE OF VISIT:

No. 1 .... No. 2 .... No. 3 ....

LOOKED IN MEDICINE CABINET?

☐ Yes, of course   ☐ No, of course not

BATHROOM DOODLE

☐ Crap   ☐ Not crap

LENGTH OF VISIT:

....

Hours   Minutes   Seconds

TIME SPENT GAZING IN MIRROR:

....

☐ Consciously   ☐ Unconsciously

THOUGHTS DURING THIS VISIT:

- ☐ The past   ☐ Business at hand
- ☐ The future   ☐ Other

REPORT CARD	A	B	C	D	F
Ambience					
Cleanliness					
Comfort					
Toilet Tissue					
Amenities					
Lighting					
Privacy					
OVERALL					

Memorable Moments: _____

_____

_____

_____

_____

_____

Additional Sentiments: _____

_____

_____

_____

_____

_____

Welcome to My Bathroom

DATE OF VISIT: ....

TIME OF VISIT: .... AM / PM

SONG THAT BEST DESCRIBES THIS BATHROOM VISIT:

☐ "More Than a Feeling"
☐ "Push It"
☐ "The Sound of Silence"
☐ "Hurts So Good"
☐ "Blowin' in the Wind"
☐ "Good Vibrations"
☐ "Ring of Fire"
☐ ....

BATHROOM ACTIVITY BAR GRAPH
Shade in the amount of time spent on various activities.

A LONG TIME

A LITTLE TIME

NO TIME

SITTING : THINKING

SIGN IN, PLEASE

PURPOSE OF VISIT:

No. 1 .... No. 2 .... No. 3 ....

LOOKED IN MEDICINE CABINET?

☐ Yes, of course   ☐ No, of course not

BATHROOM DOODLE

☐ Crap   ☐ Not crap

LENGTH OF VISIT:

....
Hours   Minutes   Seconds

TIME SPENT GAZING IN MIRROR:

....
☐ Consciously   ☐ Unconsciously

THOUGHTS DURING THIS VISIT:

☐ The past   ☐ Business at hand
☐ The future   ☐ Other

REPORT CARD	A	B	C	D	F
Ambience					
Cleanliness					
Comfort					
Toilet Tissue					
Amenities					
Lighting					
Privacy					
OVERALL					

Memorable Moments: _____

_____

_____

_____

_____

_____

Additional Sentiments: _____

_____

_____

_____

_____

_____

Welcome to My Bathroom

DATE OF VISIT: ....

TIME OF VISIT: .... AM / PM

SONG THAT BEST DESCRIBES THIS BATHROOM VISIT:

- ☐ "More Than a Feeling"
- ☐ "Push It"
- ☐ "The Sound of Silence"
- ☐ "Hurts So Good"
- ☐ "Blowin' in the Wind"
- ☐ "Good Vibrations"
- ☐ "Ring of Fire"
- ☐ ....

BATHROOM ACTIVITY BAR GRAPH
Shade in the amount of time spent on various activities.

A LONG TIME

A LITTLE TIME

NO TIME

| SITTING | THINKING |

SIGN IN, PLEASE

PURPOSE OF VISIT:

No. 1 .... No. 2 .... No. 3 ....

LOOKED IN MEDICINE CABINET?

☐ Yes, of course   ☐ No, of course not

BATHROOM DOODLE

☐ Crap   ☐ Not crap

LENGTH OF VISIT:

....

Hours   Minutes   Seconds

TIME SPENT GAZING IN MIRROR:

....

☐ Consciously   ☐ Unconsciously

THOUGHTS DURING THIS VISIT:

- ☐ The past   ☐ Business at hand
- ☐ The future   ☐ Other

REPORT CARD	A	B	C	D	F
Ambience					
Cleanliness					
Comfort					
Toilet Tissue					
Amenities					
Lighting					
Privacy					
OVERALL					

Memorable Moments: _____

_____

_____

_____

_____

_____

Additional Sentiments: _____

_____

_____

_____

_____

_____

Welcome to My Bathroom

DATE OF VISIT: ....
TIME OF VISIT: .... AM / PM

SONG THAT BEST DESCRIBES THIS BATHROOM VISIT:

- ☐ "More Than a Feeling"
- ☐ "Push It"
- ☐ "The Sound of Silence"
- ☐ "Hurts So Good"
- ☐ "Blowin' in the Wind"
- ☐ "Good Vibrations"
- ☐ "Ring of Fire"
- ☐ ....

BATHROOM ACTIVITY BAR GRAPH
Shade in the amount of time spent on various activities.

A LONG TIME

A LITTLE TIME

NO TIME

| SITTING | THINKING |

SIGN IN, PLEASE

PURPOSE OF VISIT:

No. 1 .... No. 2 .... No. 3 ....

LOOKED IN MEDICINE CABINET?

☐ Yes, of course   ☐ No, of course not

BATHROOM DOODLE

☐ Crap   ☐ Not crap

LENGTH OF VISIT:

....
Hours   Minutes   Seconds

TIME SPENT GAZING IN MIRROR:

....
☐ Consciously   ☐ Unconsciously

THOUGHTS DURING THIS VISIT:
- ☐ The past   ☐ Business at hand
- ☐ The future   ☐ Other

REPORT CARD	A	B	C	D	F
Ambience					
Cleanliness					
Comfort					
Toilet Tissue					
Amenities					
Lighting					
Privacy					
OVERALL					

Memorable Moments: _____

_____
_____
_____
_____
_____

Additional Sentiments: _____

_____
_____
_____
_____
_____

Welcome to My Bathroom

DATE OF VISIT: ....

TIME OF VISIT: .... AM / PM

SONG THAT BEST DESCRIBES THIS BATHROOM VISIT:

- ☐ "More Than a Feeling"
- ☐ "Push It"
- ☐ "The Sound of Silence"
- ☐ "Hurts So Good"
- ☐ "Blowin' in the Wind"
- ☐ "Good Vibrations"
- ☐ "Ring of Fire"
- ☐ ....

BATHROOM ACTIVITY BAR GRAPH
Shade in the amount of time spent on various activities.

A LONG TIME

A LITTLE TIME

NO TIME

SITTING | THINKING

SIGN IN, PLEASE

PURPOSE OF VISIT:

No. 1 .... No. 2 .... No. 3 ....

LOOKED IN MEDICINE CABINET?

☐ Yes, of course   ☐ No, of course not

BATHROOM DOODLE

☐ Crap   ☐ Not crap

LENGTH OF VISIT:

Hours   Minutes   Seconds

TIME SPENT GAZING IN MIRROR:

....

☐ Consciously   ☐ Unconsciously

THOUGHTS DURING THIS VISIT:

☐ The past   ☐ Business at hand
☐ The future   ☐ Other

REPORT CARD	A	B	C	D	F
Ambience					
Cleanliness					
Comfort					
Toilet Tissue					
Amenities					
Lighting					
Privacy					
OVERALL					

Memorable Moments: _____

_____

_____

_____

_____

_____

Additional Sentiments: _____

_____

_____

_____

_____

_____

Welcome to My Bathroom

DATE OF VISIT: ....
TIME OF VISIT: .... AM / PM

SONG THAT BEST DESCRIBES THIS BATHROOM VISIT:
- ☐ "More Than a Feeling"
- ☐ "Push It"
- ☐ "The Sound of Silence"
- ☐ "Hurts So Good"
- ☐ "Blowin' in the Wind"
- ☐ "Good Vibrations"
- ☐ "Ring of Fire"
- ☐ ....

BATHROOM ACTIVITY BAR GRAPH
Shade in the amount of time spent on various activities.

A LONG TIME

A LITTLE TIME

NO TIME

| SITTING | THINKING |

SIGN IN, PLEASE

PURPOSE OF VISIT:
No. 1 .... No. 2 .... No. 3 ....

LOOKED IN MEDICINE CABINET?
☐ Yes, of course   ☐ No, of course not

BATHROOM DOODLE

☐ Crap   ☐ Not crap

LENGTH OF VISIT:

....
Hours   Minutes   Seconds

TIME SPENT GAZING IN MIRROR:

....
☐ Consciously   ☐ Unconsciously

THOUGHTS DURING THIS VISIT:
☐ The past   ☐ Business at hand
☐ The future   ☐ Other

REPORT CARD	A	B	C	D	F
Ambience					
Cleanliness					
Comfort					
Toilet Tissue					
Amenities					
Lighting					
Privacy					
OVERALL					

Memorable Moments: _____

_____

_____

_____

_____

_____

Additional Sentiments: _____

_____

_____

_____

_____

_____

Welcome to My Bathroom

DATE OF VISIT: ....

TIME OF VISIT: .... AM / PM

SONG THAT BEST DESCRIBES THIS BATHROOM VISIT:

- ☐ "More Than a Feeling"
- ☐ "Push It"
- ☐ "The Sound of Silence"
- ☐ "Hurts So Good"
- ☐ "Blowin' in the Wind"
- ☐ "Good Vibrations"
- ☐ "Ring of Fire"
- ☐ ....

BATHROOM ACTIVITY BAR GRAPH

Shade in the amount of time spent on various activities.

A LONG TIME	
A LITTLE TIME	
NO TIME	
	SITTING : THINKING

SIGN IN, PLEASE

PURPOSE OF VISIT:

No. 1 .... No. 2 .... No. 3 ....

LOOKED IN MEDICINE CABINET?

☐ Yes, of course   ☐ No, of course not

BATHROOM DOODLE

☐ Crap   ☐ Not crap

LENGTH OF VISIT:

....

Hours   Minutes   Seconds

TIME SPENT GAZING IN MIRROR:

....

☐ Consciously   ☐ Unconsciously

THOUGHTS DURING THIS VISIT:

- ☐ The past
- ☐ The future
- ☐ Business at hand
- ☐ Other

REPORT CARD	A	B	C	D	F
Ambience					
Cleanliness					
Comfort					
Toilet Tissue					
Amenities					
Lighting					
Privacy					
OVERALL					

Memorable Moments: _____

_____

_____

_____

_____

_____

Additional Sentiments: _____

_____

_____

_____

_____

_____

Welcome to My Bathroom

DATE OF VISIT: ....

TIME OF VISIT: .... AM / PM

SONG THAT BEST DESCRIBES THIS BATHROOM VISIT:

- ☐ "More Than a Feeling"
- ☐ "Push It"
- ☐ "The Sound of Silence"
- ☐ "Hurts So Good"
- ☐ "Blowin' in the Wind"
- ☐ "Good Vibrations"
- ☐ "Ring of Fire"
- ☐ ....

BATHROOM ACTIVITY BAR GRAPH

Shade in the amount of time spent on various activities.

A LONG TIME	
A LITTLE TIME	
NO TIME	
	SITTING : THINKING

SIGN IN, PLEASE

PURPOSE OF VISIT:

No. 1 .... No. 2 .... No. 3 ....

LOOKED IN MEDICINE CABINET?

☐ Yes, of course   ☐ No, of course not

BATHROOM DOODLE

☐ Crap   ☐ Not crap

LENGTH OF VISIT:

....

Hours   Minutes   Seconds

TIME SPENT GAZING IN MIRROR:

....

☐ Consciously   ☐ Unconsciously

THOUGHTS DURING THIS VISIT:

- ☐ The past   ☐ Business at hand
- ☐ The future   ☐ Other

REPORT CARD	A	B	C	D	F
Ambience					
Cleanliness					
Comfort					
Toilet Tissue					
Amenities					
Lighting					
Privacy					
OVERALL					

Memorable Moments: _____

_____

_____

_____

_____

_____

Additional Sentiments: _____

_____

_____

_____

_____

_____

Welcome to My Bathroom

DATE OF VISIT: ....

TIME OF VISIT: .... AM / PM

SONG THAT BEST DESCRIBES THIS BATHROOM VISIT:

☐ "More Than a Feeling"
☐ "Push It"
☐ "The Sound of Silence"
☐ "Hurts So Good"
☐ "Blowin' in the Wind"
☐ "Good Vibrations"
☐ "Ring of Fire"
☐ ....

BATHROOM ACTIVITY BAR GRAPH
Shade in the amount of time spent on various activities.

A LONG
TIME

A LITTLE
TIME

NO TIME

| SITTING | THINKING |

SIGN IN, PLEASE

PURPOSE OF VISIT:

No. 1 ....   No. 2 ....   No. 3 ....

LOOKED IN MEDICINE CABINET?

☐ Yes, of course   ☐ No, of course not

BATHROOM DOODLE

☐ Crap   ☐ Not crap

LENGTH OF VISIT:

....

Hours   Minutes   Seconds

TIME SPENT GAZING IN MIRROR:

....

☐ Consciously   ☐ Unconsciously

THOUGHTS DURING THIS VISIT:

☐ The past   ☐ Business at hand
☐ The future   ☐ Other

REPORT CARD	A	B	C	D	F
Ambience					
Cleanliness					
Comfort					
Toilet Tissue					
Amenities					
Lighting					
Privacy					
OVERALL					

Memorable Moments: _____

_____

_____

_____

_____

_____

Additional Sentiments: _____

_____

_____

_____

_____

_____

Welcome to My Bathroom

DATE OF VISIT: ....

TIME OF VISIT: .... AM / PM

SONG THAT BEST DESCRIBES THIS BATHROOM VISIT:

☐ "More Than a Feeling"
☐ "Push It"
☐ "The Sound of Silence"
☐ "Hurts So Good"
☐ "Blowin' in the Wind"
☐ "Good Vibrations"
☐ "Ring of Fire"
☐ ....

BATHROOM ACTIVITY BAR GRAPH
Shade in the amount of time spent on various activities.

A LONG TIME

A LITTLE TIME

NO TIME

| SITTING | THINKING |

SIGN IN, PLEASE

PURPOSE OF VISIT:

No. 1 .... No. 2 .... No. 3 ....

LOOKED IN MEDICINE CABINET?

☐ Yes, of course   ☐ No, of course not

BATHROOM DOODLE

☐ Crap   ☐ Not crap

LENGTH OF VISIT:

....

Hours   Minutes   Seconds

TIME SPENT GAZING IN MIRROR:

....

☐ Consciously   ☐ Unconsciously

THOUGHTS DURING THIS VISIT:
☐ The past   ☐ Business at hand
☐ The future   ☐ Other

REPORT CARD	A	B	C	D	F
Ambience					
Cleanliness					
Comfort					
Toilet Tissue					
Amenities					
Lighting					
Privacy					
OVERALL					

Memorable Moments: _____

_____

_____

_____

_____

_____

Additional Sentiments: _____

_____

_____

_____

_____

_____

Welcome to My Bathroom

DATE OF VISIT: ....

TIME OF VISIT: .... AM / PM

SONG THAT BEST DESCRIBES THIS BATHROOM VISIT:

- ☐ "More Than a Feeling"
- ☐ "Push It"
- ☐ "The Sound of Silence"
- ☐ "Hurts So Good"
- ☐ "Blowin' in the Wind"
- ☐ "Good Vibrations"
- ☐ "Ring of Fire"
- ☐ ....

BATHROOM ACTIVITY BAR GRAPH
Shade in the amount of time spent on various activities.

A LONG TIME

A LITTLE TIME

NO TIME

| SITTING | THINKING |

SIGN IN, PLEASE

PURPOSE OF VISIT:

No. 1 .... No. 2 .... No. 3 ....

LOOKED IN MEDICINE CABINET?

☐ Yes, of course   ☐ No, of course not

BATHROOM DOODLE

☐ Crap   ☐ Not crap

LENGTH OF VISIT:

....

Hours   Minutes   Seconds

TIME SPENT GAZING IN MIRROR:

....

☐ Consciously   ☐ Unconsciously

THOUGHTS DURING THIS VISIT:

☐ The past   ☐ Business at hand
☐ The future   ☐ Other

REPORT CARD	A	B	C	D	F
Ambience					
Cleanliness					
Comfort					
Toilet Tissue					
Amenities					
Lighting					
Privacy					
OVERALL					

Memorable Moments: _____

_____

_____

_____

_____

_____

Additional Sentiments: _____

_____

_____

_____

_____

_____

Welcome to My Bathroom

DATE OF VISIT: ....
TIME OF VISIT: .... AM / PM

SONG THAT BEST DESCRIBES THIS BATHROOM VISIT:

- ☐ "More Than a Feeling"
- ☐ "Push It"
- ☐ "The Sound of Silence"
- ☐ "Hurts So Good"
- ☐ "Blowin' in the Wind"
- ☐ "Good Vibrations"
- ☐ "Ring of Fire"
- ☐ ....

BATHROOM ACTIVITY BAR GRAPH
Shade in the amount of time spent on various activities.

A LONG TIME

A LITTLE TIME

NO TIME

| SITTING | THINKING |

SIGN IN, PLEASE

PURPOSE OF VISIT:

No. 1 .... No. 2 .... No. 3 ....

LOOKED IN MEDICINE CABINET?

☐ Yes, of course ☐ No, of course not

BATHROOM DOODLE

☐ Crap ☐ Not crap

LENGTH OF VISIT:

....
Hours   Minutes   Seconds

TIME SPENT GAZING IN MIRROR:

....
☐ Consciously ☐ Unconsciously

THOUGHTS DURING THIS VISIT:
- ☐ The past
- ☐ Business at hand
- ☐ The future
- ☐ Other

REPORT CARD	A	B	C	D	F
Ambience					
Cleanliness					
Comfort					
Toilet Tissue					
Amenities					
Lighting					
Privacy					
OVERALL					

Memorable Moments: _____

_____

_____

_____

_____

Additional Sentiments: _____

_____

_____

_____

_____

Welcome to My Bathroom

DATE OF VISIT: ....

TIME OF VISIT: .... AM / PM

SONG THAT BEST DESCRIBES THIS BATHROOM VISIT:

☐ "More Than a Feeling"
☐ "Push It"
☐ "The Sound of Silence"
☐ "Hurts So Good"
☐ "Blowin' in the Wind"
☐ "Good Vibrations"
☐ "Ring of Fire"
☐ ....

BATHROOM ACTIVITY BAR GRAPH
Shade in the amount of time spent on various activities.

A LONG TIME

A LITTLE TIME

NO TIME

| SITTING | THINKING |

SIGN IN, PLEASE

PURPOSE OF VISIT:

No. 1 .... No. 2 .... No. 3 ....

LOOKED IN MEDICINE CABINET?

☐ Yes, of course ☐ No, of course not

BATHROOM DOODLE

☐ Crap ☐ Not crap

LENGTH OF VISIT:

....

Hours   Minutes   Seconds

TIME SPENT GAZING IN MIRROR:

....

☐ Consciously ☐ Unconsciously

THOUGHTS DURING THIS VISIT:

☐ The past ☐ Business at hand
☐ The future ☐ Other

REPORT CARD	A	B	C	D	F
Ambience					
Cleanliness					
Comfort					
Toilet Tissue					
Amenities					
Lighting					
Privacy					
OVERALL					

Memorable Moments: _____

_____

_____

_____

_____

_____

Additional Sentiments: _____

_____

_____

_____

_____

_____

Welcome to My Bathroom

DATE OF VISIT: ....

TIME OF VISIT: .... AM / PM

SONG THAT BEST DESCRIBES THIS BATHROOM VISIT:

- ☐ "More Than a Feeling"
- ☐ "Push It"
- ☐ "The Sound of Silence"
- ☐ "Hurts So Good"
- ☐ "Blowin' in the Wind"
- ☐ "Good Vibrations"
- ☐ "Ring of Fire"
- ☐ ....

BATHROOM ACTIVITY BAR GRAPH

Shade in the amount of time spent on various activities.

A LONG TIME

A LITTLE TIME

NO TIME

SITTING | THINKING

SIGN IN, PLEASE

PURPOSE OF VISIT:

No. 1 .... No. 2 .... No. 3 ....

LOOKED IN MEDICINE CABINET?

☐ Yes, of course ☐ No, of course not

BATHROOM DOODLE

☐ Crap ☐ Not crap

LENGTH OF VISIT:

....

Hours   Minutes   Seconds

TIME SPENT GAZING IN MIRROR:

....

☐ Consciously ☐ Unconsciously

THOUGHTS DURING THIS VISIT:

- ☐ The past ☐ Business at hand
- ☐ The future ☐ Other

REPORT CARD	A	B	C	D	F
Ambience					
Cleanliness					
Comfort					
Toilet Tissue					
Amenities					
Lighting					
Privacy					
OVERALL					

Memorable Moments: _____

_____

_____

_____

_____

_____

Additional Sentiments: _____

_____

_____

_____

_____

_____

Welcome to My Bathroom

DATE OF VISIT: ....

TIME OF VISIT: .... AM / PM

SONG THAT BEST DESCRIBES THIS BATHROOM VISIT:

- ☐ "More Than a Feeling"
- ☐ "Push It"
- ☐ "The Sound of Silence"
- ☐ "Hurts So Good"
- ☐ "Blowin' in the Wind"
- ☐ "Good Vibrations"
- ☐ "Ring of Fire"
- ☐ ....

BATHROOM ACTIVITY BAR GRAPH

Shade in the amount of time spent on various activities.

A LONG TIME

A LITTLE TIME

NO TIME

| SITTING | THINKING |

SIGN IN, PLEASE

PURPOSE OF VISIT:

No. 1 .... No. 2 .... No. 3 ....

LOOKED IN MEDICINE CABINET?

☐ Yes, of course   ☐ No, of course not

BATHROOM DOODLE

☐ Crap   ☐ Not crap

LENGTH OF VISIT:

....

Hours   Minutes   Seconds

TIME SPENT GAZING IN MIRROR:

....

☐ Consciously   ☐ Unconsciously

THOUGHTS DURING THIS VISIT:

- ☐ The past   ☐ Business at hand
- ☐ The future   ☐ Other

REPORT CARD	A	B	C	D	F
Ambience					
Cleanliness					
Comfort					
Toilet Tissue					
Amenities					
Lighting					
Privacy					
OVERALL					

Memorable Moments: _____

_____

_____

_____

_____

Additional Sentiments: _____

_____

_____

_____

_____

Welcome to My Bathroom

DATE OF VISIT: ....

TIME OF VISIT: .... AM / PM

SONG THAT BEST DESCRIBES THIS BATHROOM VISIT:

☐ "More Than a Feeling"
☐ "Push It"
☐ "The Sound of Silence"
☐ "Hurts So Good"
☐ "Blowin' in the Wind"
☐ "Good Vibrations"
☐ "Ring of Fire"
☐ ....

BATHROOM ACTIVITY BAR GRAPH
Shade in the amount of time spent on various activities.

A LONG TIME

A LITTLE TIME

NO TIME

SITTING | THINKING

SIGN IN, PLEASE

PURPOSE OF VISIT:

No. 1 .... No. 2 .... No. 3 ....

LOOKED IN MEDICINE CABINET?

☐ Yes, of course   ☐ No, of course not

BATHROOM DOODLE

☐ Crap   ☐ Not crap

LENGTH OF VISIT:

....

Hours   Minutes   Seconds

TIME SPENT GAZING IN MIRROR:

....

☐ Consciously   ☐ Unconsciously

THOUGHTS DURING THIS VISIT:

☐ The past   ☐ Business at hand
☐ The future   ☐ Other

REPORT CARD	A	B	C	D	F
Ambience					
Cleanliness					
Comfort					
Toilet Tissue					
Amenities					
Lighting					
Privacy					
OVERALL					

Memorable Moments:

Additional Sentiments:

Welcome to My Bathroom

DATE OF VISIT: Mar. 31/16

TIME OF VISIT: 3:24 .... AM / PM

SONG THAT BEST DESCRIBES THIS BATHROOM VISIT:

- ☐ "More Than a Feeling"
- ☒ "Push It"
- ☐ "The Sound of Silence"
- ☐ "Hurts So Good"
- ☐ "Blowin' in the Wind"
- ☐ "Good Vibrations"
- ☐ "Ring of Fire"
- ☐ ....

BATHROOM ACTIVITY BAR GRAPH

Shade in the amount of time spent on various activities.

A LONG TIME

A LITTLE TIME

NO TIME

SITTING | THINKING

SIGN IN, PLEASE

Lily Johnston

PURPOSE OF VISIT:

No. 1 .... No. 2 ..✓......... No. 3 ....

LOOKED IN MEDICINE CABINET?

☐ Yes, of course ☒ No, of course not

BATHROOM DOODLE

Lily   Lilia

Lilia

Lilia

☒ Crap ☐ Not crap

LENGTH OF VISIT:

Hours   Minutes   Seconds

TIME SPENT GAZING IN MIRROR:

☐ Consciously ☐ Unconsciously

THOUGHTS DURING THIS VISIT:

- ☐ The past
- ☐ The future
- ☐ Business at hand
- ☐ Other

REPORT CARD	A	B	C	D	F
Ambience					
Cleanliness					
Comfort					
Toilet Tissue					
Amenities					
Lighting					
Privacy					
OVERALL					

Memorable Moments: _____
_____
_____
_____
_____
_____

Additional Sentiments: _____
_____
_____
_____
_____
_____

Welcome to My Bathroom

DATE OF VISIT: March 22/16
TIME OF VISIT: 11:45 AM / PM

SIGN IN, PLEASE

LENGTH OF VISIT:

.... ✓ ....
Hours   Minutes   Seconds

SONG THAT BEST DESCRIBES THIS BATHROOM VISIT:

- ☐ "More Than a Feeling"
- ☐ "Push It"
- ☐ "The Sound of Silence"
- ☐ "Hurts So Good"
- ☐ "Blowin' in the Wind"
- ☐ "Good Vibrations"
- ☐ "Ring of Fire"
- ☐ ....

PURPOSE OF VISIT:

No. 1 ....   No. 2 ....✓.......   No. 3 ....

LOOKED IN MEDICINE CABINET?

☐ Yes, of course   ☑ No, of course not

BATHROOM DOODLE

☑ Crap   ☐ Not crap

TIME SPENT GAZING IN MIRROR:

didn't do that

☐ Consciously   ☐ Unconsciously

THOUGHTS DURING THIS VISIT:

- ☑ The past   ☑ Business at hand
- ☑ The future   ☐ Other

BATHROOM ACTIVITY BAR GRAPH

Shade in the amount of time spent on various activities.

A LONG TIME

A LITTLE TIME

NO TIME

SITTING | THINKING

REPORT CARD	A	B	C	D	F
Ambience	A				
Cleanliness	A				
Comfort	F				
Toilet Tissue	A				
Amenities	2				
Lighting	A				
Privacy	A				
OVERALL					

Memorable Moments: _____

_____

_____

_____

_____

Additional Sentiments: _____

_____

_____

_____

_____

Welcome to My Bathroom

DATE OF VISIT: Nov. 11/18

TIME OF VISIT: 11:00   AM / PM

SONG THAT BEST DESCRIBES THIS BATHROOM VISIT:

- ☐ "More Than a Feeling"
- ☑ "Push It"
- ☐ "The Sound of Silence"
- ☐ "Hurts So Good"
- ☐ "Blowin' in the Wind"
- ☐ "Good Vibrations"
- ☐ "Ring of Fire"
- ☐ ....

BATHROOM ACTIVITY BAR GRAPH
Shade in the amount of time spent on various activities.

A LONG TIME

A LITTLE TIME

NO TIME

| SITTING | THINKING |

SIGN IN, PLEASE

PURPOSE OF VISIT:

No. 1 .... No. 2 .... No. 3 ....

LOOKED IN MEDICINE CABINET?

☐ Yes, of course   ☐ No, of course not

BATHROOM DOODLE

☑ Crap   ☐ Not crap

LENGTH OF VISIT:

....

Hours   Minutes   Seconds

TIME SPENT GAZING IN MIRROR:

Didnt do that

☐ Consciously   ☑ Unconsciously

THOUGHTS DURING THIS VISIT:

- ☐ The past
- ☑ The future
- ☐ Business at hand
- ☐ Other

REPORT CARD	A	B	C	D	F
Ambience	6				
Cleanliness	6				
Comfort	6				
Toilet Tissue	6				
Amenities	6				
Lighting	6				
Privacy	6				
OVERALL					

Memorable Moments: _____

_____

_____

_____

_____

Additional Sentiments: _____

_____

_____

_____

_____

Welcome to My Bathroom

DATE OF VISIT: August

TIME OF VISIT: PM   AM / PM

SONG THAT BEST DESCRIBES THIS BATHROOM VISIT:

☐ "More Than a Feeling"
☑ "Push It"
☐ "The Sound of Silence"
☐ "Hurts So Good"
☐ "Blowin' in the Wind"
☐ "Good Vibrations"
☐ "Ring of Fire"
☐ ....

BATHROOM ACTIVITY BAR GRAPH
Shade in the amount of time spent on various activities.

A LONG TIME

A LITTLE TIME

NO TIME

SITTING | THINKING

SIGN IN, PLEASE

PURPOSE OF VISIT:

No. 1 ......✓...... No. 2 ......✓...... No. 3 ....

LOOKED IN MEDICINE CABINET?

☐ Yes, of course   ☑ No, of course not

BATHROOM DOODLE

☑ Crap   ☐ Not crap

LENGTH OF VISIT:

...............✓...............

Hours   Minutes   Seconds

TIME SPENT GAZING IN MIRROR:

Didnt Do that

☐ Consciously   ☐ Unconsciously

THOUGHTS DURING THIS VISIT:

☐ The past   ☐ Business at hand
☐ The future   ☑ Other

REPORT CARD	A	B	C	D	F
Ambience					
Cleanliness					
Comfort					
Toilet Tissue					
Amenities					
Lighting					
Privacy					
OVERALL